101 WISDOM KEYS

BY MIKE MURDOCK

Wisdom is the principal thing; therefore get wisdom: and with all thy getting get understanding.
Proverbs 4:7

Wisdom International
P.O. Box 747
Dallas, Texas 75221

Unless otherwise indicated, all Scripture quotations are taken from the *King James Version* of the Bible.

101 Wisdom Keys
ISBN 1-56394-010-8
Copyright © 1994 by Mike Murdock
P.O. Box 99
Denton. Texas 76202

Published by
Wisdom International
P.O. Box 747
Dallas, Texas 75221

*Never Complain About
What You Permit.*

1

*The Problem That
Infuriates You The Most Is
The Problem That God Has
Assigned You To Solve.*

2

*Those Who Unlock Your
Compassion Are Those
To Whom You Have
Been Assigned.*

3

*What You Are Willing
To Walk Away From
Determines What God
Will Bring To You.*

4

5

The Secret Of Your Future Is Hidden In Your Daily Routine.

6

Your Rewards In Life Are Determined By The Problems You Solve For Others.

7

When You Want Something You Have Never Had, You Have Got To Do Something You Have Never Done.

8

All Men Fall... The Great Ones Get Back Up.

Intolerance Of Your Present Creates Your Future.

9

Those Who Cannot Increase You Will Inevitably Decrease You.

10

You Will Never Leave Where You Are Until You Decide Where You Would Rather Be.

11

You Will Only Have Significant Success With Something That Is An Obsession.

12

13 *Give Another What He Cannot Find Anywhere Else And He Will Keep Returning.*

14 *Your Assignment Is Not Your Decision But Your Discovery.*

15 *When Fatigue Walks In, Faith Walks Out.*

16 *If What You Hold In Your Hand Is Not Enough To Be Your Harvest, Make It Your Seed.*

*You Will Never Change
What You Believe Until
Your Belief System Cannot
Produce Something You
Want.*

17

*You Will Only Be Pursued
For The Problems You
Solve.*

18

*Champions Are Willing To
Do Things They Hate To
Create Something Else
They Love.*

19

*You Will Never Possess
What You Are Unwilling
To Pursue.*

20

7

*The Only Reason Men Fail
Is Broken Focus.*

*Stop Looking At Where
You Have Been And Start
Looking At Where You
Can Be.*

*You Will Only Be
Remembered For Two
Things; The Problems
You Solve Or The Ones
You Create.*

*Those Who Transfer
Knowledge Are Also
Capable Of Transferring
Error.*

Your Seed Is The Only Influence You Have Over Your Future.

25

Loneliness Is Not The Absence Of Affection, But The Absence Of Direction.

26

You Cannot Be What You Are Not, But You Can Become What You Are Not.

27

False Accusation Is The Last Stage Before Supernatural Promotion.

28

29 *Your Seed Is A Photograph Of Your Faith.*

30 *What You Repeatedly Hear You Will Eventually Believe.*

31 *God Never Consults Your Past To Determine Your Future.*

32 *Satan Always Attacks Those Next In Line For A Promotion.*

*Power Is The Ability
To Walk Away From
Something Else You
Desire... To Protect
Something You Love.*

33

*Anything That Does Not
Change You Is Unnecessary
In Your Life.*

34

*When You Discover Your
Assignment, You Will
Discover Your Enemy.*

35

*What You Respect,
You Will Attract.*

36

37 *Men Decide Their Habits...
Their Habits Decide Their
Future.*

38 *You Cannot Correct What
You Are Unwilling To
Confront.*

39 *The Proof Of Desire
Is Pursuit.*

40 *Crisis Always Occurs At
The Curve Of Change.*

If Time Heals,
God Is Unnecessary.

41

Your Seed Is Anything That
Benefits Another While
Your Harvest Is Anything
That Benefits You.

42

Satan's Favorite Entry
Point Into Your Life Is
Always Through Someone
Close To You.

43

What You Hate Reveals
What You Were Created
To Correct.

44

45 *Losers Focus On What They Are Going Through While Champions Focus On What They Are Going To.*

46 *When You Let Go Of What Is In Your Hand, God Will Let Go Of What Is In His Hand.*

47 *Pain Is Not An Enemy But Merely The Proof That One Exists.*

48 *When God Wants To Bless You, He Puts A Person In Your Life... When Satan Wants To Destroy You, He Puts A Person In Your Life.*

Currents Of Favor Begin To Flow The Moment You Solve A Problem For Someone.

49

The Seed That Leaves Your Hand Never Leaves Your Life... But Enters Your Future Where It Multiplies.

50

Each Act Of Obedience Shortens The Distance To Any Miracle You Are Pursuing.

51

The Quality Of Your Preparation Determines The Quality Of Your Performance.

52

*Champions Make Decisions
That Create The Future They
Desire... While Losers Make
Decisions That Create The
Present They Desire.*

*Creativity Is The Search
For Options; Concentration
Is The Elimination Of
Them.*

*Seed-Faith Is Sowing What
You Have Been Given To
Create What You Have
Been Promised.*

*The Seasons Of Your Life
Will Change Every Time
You Decide To Use Your
Faith.*

Someone Is Always Observing You Who Is Capable Of Greatly Blessing You.

57

Giving Is Proof That You Have Conquered Greed.

58

The Season For Research Is Not The Season For Marketing.

59

What You Fail To Master In Your Life Will Eventually Master You.

60

61 *Go Where You Are Celebrated Instead Of Where You Are Tolerated.*

62 *The Broken Become Masters At Mending.*

63 *Your Significance Is Not In Your Similarity To Another, But In Your Point Of Difference From Another.*

64 *You Will Always Pursue The Friendship That Solves Your Most Immediate Problem.*

*The Worth Of Any
Relationship Can Be
Measured By Its
Contributions To Your
Priorities.*

65

*You Will Never Conquer
What You Refuse To Hate.*

66

*Injustice Is Only As
Powerful As Your Memory
Of It.*

67

*Every Relationship In Your
Life Is A Current Moving
You Toward Your Dreams
Or Away From Them.*

68

69 *You Will Never Be Promoted Until You Have Become Over-Qualified For Your Present Assignment.*

70 *Money Is Merely A Reward For Solving Problems.*

71 *Your Reaction To Someone In Trouble Determines God's Reaction To You The Next Time You Get In Trouble.*

72 *What You Can Tolerate, You Cannot Change.*

The Waves Of Yesterday's Disobedience Will Splash On The Shores Of Today For A Season.

73

You Will Never Outgrow Warfare... You Must Simply Learn To Fight.

74

Nothing Is Ever As Bad As It First Appears.

75

The Evidence Of God's Presence Far Outweighs The Proof Of His Absence.

76

77 *Patience Is The Weapon That Forces Deception To Reveal Itself.*

78 *One Hour In The Presence Of God Will Reveal Any Flaw In Your Most Carefully Laid Plan.*

79 *Never Spend More Time On A Critic Than You Would Give To A Friend.*

80 *Those Who Do Not Respect Your Assignment Disqualify Themselves For A Relationship.*

You Will Never Reach The Palace Talking Like A Peasant.

81

Struggle Is The Proof You Have Not Yet Been Conquered.

82

Never Discuss Your Problem With Someone Incapable Of Solving It.

83

Greatness Is Not The Pursuit Of Perfection But The Pursuit Of Completion.

84

85 *Never Rewrite Your Theology To Accommodate A Tragedy.*

86 *The Greatest Quality On Earth Is The Willingness To Become.*

87 *Warfare Always Surrounds The Birth Of A Miracle.*

88 *Failure Is Not An Event, But An Opinion.*

You Are Never As Far From A Miracle As It First Appears.

89

What You See Determines What You Desire.

90

The Atmosphere You Permit Determines The Product You Produce.

91

Prosperity Is Simply Having Enough Of God's Provision To Complete His Instructions For Your Life.

92

God Will Never Advance Your Instructions Beyond Your Last Act Of Disobedience.

Anger Is The Birthplace For Solutions.

Those Who Do Not Respect Your Time Will Not Respect Your Wisdom Either.

Discontent Is The Catalyst For Change.

*Crisis Is Merely
Concentrated Information.*

97

---

*Silence Cannot Be
Misquoted.*

98

---

*Those Who Created The
Pain Of Yesterday Do Not
Control The Pleasure Of
Tomorrow.*

99

---

*When You Change Your
Focus You Will Change
Your Feelings.*

100

101

What You Make Happen For Others, God Will Make Happen For You.

Notes

_____

_____

_____

_____

_____

_____

_____

_____

_____

_____

_____

_____

_____

_____

_____

_____

_____

DECISION

Will You Accept Jesus As Your Personal Savior Today?

The Bible says, "That if thou shalt confess with thy mouth the Lord Jesus, and shall believe in thine heart that God hath raised Him from the dead, thou shalt be saved. For with the heart man believeth unto righteousness; and with the mouth confession is made unto salvation." (Rom. 10:9-10)

Pray this prayer from your heart today!

"Dear Jesus, I believe that You died for me and rose again on the third day. I confess that I am a sinner...I need Your love and forgiveness. Come into my heart. Forgive my sins. I receive Your eternal life. Confirm Your love by giving me peace, joy and supernatural love for others. I confess You now as my Lord. Thank you for my salvation! I walk in Your peace and joy from this day forward. Amen."

DR. MIKE MURDOCK

is in tremendous demand as one of the most dynamic speakers in America today.

More than 14,000 audiences in 38 countries have attended his meetings and seminars. Hundreds of invitations come to him from churches, colleges, and business corporations. He is a noted author of over 115 books, including the best seller, "The Leadership Secrets of Jesus" and "Secrets of The Richest Man Who Ever Lived." Thousands view his weekly television program, "Wisdom Keys with Mike Murdock." Many have attended his annual Schools of Wisdom at his headquarters, The Wisdom Center, in Denton, Texas.

Wisdom Key Partnership Pak

When you become a Wisdom Key Monthly Faith Partner, you will receive our Partnership Pak which includes:

1. Special Music Cassette
2. 101 Wisdom Keys Book
3. Partnership Coupon Book

Yes, Mike! I Want To Be Your Partner!

❏ Enclosed is my best Seed-Faith Gift of $_____

❏ I want to be a Wisdom Key Partner! Enclosed is my first Seed-Faith Gift of $_____ for the first month.

❏ Please rush my special Partnership Pak. (#PP02)

Name_____
Address _____
City _____State_____Zip_____
Phone _____

Mail To:
DR. MIKE MURDOCK
P.O. Box 99
Denton, Texas 76202
Phone 940-891-1400 • Fax 940-891-4500
www.mikemurdock.com

ORDER FORM THE MIKE MURDOCK WISDOM LIBRARY

(All books paperback unless indicated otherwise.)

QTY	CODE	BOOK TITLE	USA	TOTAL
	B01	WISDOM FOR WINNING	$10	
	B02	5 STEPS OUT OF DEPRESSION	$ 2	
	B03	THE SEX TRAP	$ 2	
	B04	10 LIES PEOPLE BELIEVE ABOUT MONEY	$ 2	
	B05	FINDING YOUR PURPOSE IN LIFE	$ 2	
	B06	CREATING TOMORROW THROUGH SEED-FAITH	$ 2	
	B07	BATTLE TECHNIQUES FOR WAR WEARY SAINTS	$ 2	
	B08	ENJOYING THE WINNING LIFE	$ 2	
	B09	FOUR FORCES/GUARANTEE CAREER SUCCESS	$ 2	
	B10	THE BRIDGE CALLED DIVORCE	$ 2	
	B11	DREAM SEEDS	$ 9	
	B12	YOUNG MINISTERS HANDBOOK	$20	
	B13	SEEDS OF WISDOM ON DREAMS AND GOALS	$ 3	
	B14	SEEDS OF WISDOM ON RELATIONSHIPS	$ 3	
	B15	SEEDS OF WISDOM ON MIRACLES	$ 3	
	B16	SEEDS OF WISDOM ON SEED-FAITH	$ 3	
	B17	SEEDS OF WISDOM ON OVERCOMING	$ 3	
	B18	SEEDS OF WISDOM ON HABITS	$ 3	
	B19	SEEDS OF WISDOM ON WARFARE	$ 3	
	B20	SEEDS OF WISDOM ON OBEDIENCE	$ 3	
	B21	SEEDS OF WISDOM ON ADVERSITY	$ 3	
	B22	SEEDS OF WISDOM ON PROSPERITY	$ 3	
	B23	SEEDS OF WISDOM ON PRAYER	$ 3	
	B24	SEEDS OF WISDOM ON FAITH TALK	$ 3	
	B25	SEEDS OF WISDOM ONE YEAR DEVOTIONAL	$10	
	B26	THE GOD BOOK	$10	
	B27	THE JESUS BOOK	$10	
	B28	THE BLESSING BIBLE	$10	
	B29	THE SURVIVAL BIBLE	$10	
	B30	TEENAGERS TOPICAL BIBLE	$ 6	
	B30L	TEENAGERS TOPICAL BIBLE (LEATHER)	$20	
	B31	ONE-MINUTE TOPICAL BIBLE	$12	
	B32	MINISTER'S TOPICAL BIBLE	$ 6	
	B33	BUSINESSMAN'S TOPICAL BIBLE	$ 6	
	B33L	BUSINESSMAN'S TOPICAL BIBLE (LEATHER)	$20	
	B34L	GRANDPARENT'S TOPICAL BIBLE (LEATHER)	$20	
	B35	FATHER'S TOPICAL BIBLE	$ 6	
	B35L	FATHER'S TOPICAL BIBLE (LEATHER)	$20	
	B36	MOTHER'S TOPICAL BIBLE	$ 6	
	B36L	MOTHER'S TOPICAL BIBLE (LEATHER)	$20	
	B37	NEW CONVERT'S BIBLE	$ 6	
	B38	THE WIDOW'S TOPICAL BIBLE	$ 6	
	B39	THE DOUBLE DIAMOND PRINCIPLE	$ 9	
	B40	WISDOM FOR CRISIS TIMES	$ 9	
	B41	THE GIFT OF WISDOM (VOLUME ONE)	$ 8	
	B42	ONE-MINUTE BUSINESSMAN'S DEVOTIONAL	$10	
	B43	ONE-MINUTE BUSINESSWOMAN'S DEVOTIONAL	$10	
	B44	31 SECRETS FOR CAREER SUCCESS	$10	
	B45	101 WISDOM KEYS	$ 7	
	B46	31 FACTS ABOUT WISDOM	$ 7	
	B47	THE COVENANT OF 58 BLESSINGS	$ 8	
	B48	31 KEYS TO A NEW BEGINNING	$ 7	
	B49	31 SECRETS OF THE PROVERBS 31 WOMAN	$ 7	
	B50	ONE-MINUTE POCKET BIBLE FOR ACHIEVERS	$ 5	
	B51	ONE-MINUTE POCKET BIBLE FOR FATHERS	$ 5	
	B52	ONE-MINUTE POCKET BIBLE FOR MOTHERS	$ 5	

MAIL FORM TO:

The Wisdom Center • P.O. Box 99 • Denton, TX 76202

Phone 940-891-1400 • Fax 940-891-4500 • www.mikemurdock.com

Qty	Code	Book Title	USA	Total
	B53	ONE-MINUTE POCKET BIBLE FOR TEENAGERS	$ 5	
	B54	ONE-MINUTE DAILY DEVOTIONAL (HARDBACK)	$14	
	B55	20 KEYS TO A HAPPIER MARRIAGE	$ 2	
	B56	HOW TO TURN MISTAKES INTO MIRACLES	$ 2	
	B57	31 SECRETS OF THE UNFORGETTABLE WOMAN	$ 9	
	B58	MENTOR'S MANNA ON ATTITUDE	$ 2	
	B59	THE MAKING OF A CHAMPION	$ 6	
	B60	ONE-MINUTE POCKET BIBLE FOR MEN	$ 5	
	B61	ONE-MINUTE POCKET BIBLE FOR WOMEN	$ 5	
	B62	ONE-MINUTE POCKET BIBLE/BUS. PROFESSIONALS	$ 5	
	B63	ONE-MINUTE POCKET BIBLE FOR TRUCKERS	$ 5	
	B64	MENTOR'S MANNA ON ACHIEVEMENT	$ 2	
	B65	MENTOR'S MANNA ON ADVERSITY	$ 2	
	B66	GREED, GOLD AND GIVING	$ 2	
	B67	GIFT OF WISDOM FOR CHAMPIONS	$ 8	
	B68	GIFT OF WISDOM FOR ACHIEVERS	$ 8	
	B69	MENTOR'S MANNA ON THE SECRET PLACE	$ 2	
	B70	GIFT OF WISDOM FOR MOTHERS	$ 8	
	B71	WISDOM - GOD'S GOLDEN KEY TO SUCCESS	$ 7	
	B72	THE DOUBLE DIAMOND DAILY DEVOTIONAL	$12	
	B73	MENTOR'S MANNA ON ABILITIES	$ 2	
	B74	THE ASSIGNMENT: DREAM/DESTINY #1	$10	
	B75	THE ASSIGNMENT: ANOINTING/ADVERSITY #2	$10	
	B76	THE ASSIGNMENT: TRIALS/TRIUMPHS #3	$10	
	B77	THE ASSIGNMENT: PAIN/PASSION #4	$10	
	B78	WISDOM KEYS FOR A POWERFUL PRAYER LIFE	$ 2	
	B79	7 OBSTACLES TO ABUNDANT SUCCESS	$ 2	
	B80	THE GREATEST SUCCESS HABIT ON EARTH	$ 2	
	B81	BORN TO TASTE THE GRAPES	$ 2	
	B82	31 REASONS PEOPLE DO NOT RECEIVE THEIR FINANCIAL HARVEST	$12	
	B83	GIFT OF WISDOM FOR WIVES	$ 8	
	B84	GIFT OF WISDOM FOR HUSBANDS	$ 8	
	B85	GIFT OF WISDOM FOR TEENAGERS	$ 8	
	B86	GIFT OF WISDOM FOR LEADERS	$ 8	
	B87	GIFT OF WISDOM FOR GRADUATES	$ 8	
	B88	GIFT OF WISDOM FOR BRIDES	$ 8	
	B89	GIFT OF WISDOM FOR GROOMS	$ 8	
	B90	GIFT OF WISDOM FOR MINISTERS	$ 8	
	B91	THE LEADERSHIP SECRETS OF JESUS (HDBK)	$15	
	B92	SECRETS OF THE JOURNEY (VOL. 1)	$ 5	
	B93	SECRETS OF THE JOURNEY (VOL. 2)	$ 5	
	B94	SECRETS OF THE JOURNEY (VOL. 3)	$ 5	
	B95	SECRETS OF THE JOURNEY (VOL. 4)	$ 5	

☐ CASH ☐ CHECK ☐ MONEY ORDER

☐ CREDIT CARD # ☐ VISA ☐ MC ☐ AMEX

EXPIRATION DATE [ ][ ][ ][ ] *SORRY NO C.O.D.'s*

SIGNATURE _____

TOTAL PAGE 2	$
TOTAL PAGE 1	$
*ADD SHIPPING 10% USA / 20% OTHERS	$
CANADA CURRENCY DIFFERENCE ADD 20%	$
TOTAL ENCLOSED	$

PLEASE PRINT

Name [| | | | | | | | | | | | | | | | |]

Address [| | | | | | | | | | | | | | | | |]

City [| | | | | | | | | | State | Zip | | | | |]

Phone (| | |) | | | - | | | |

Your Search Is Over.

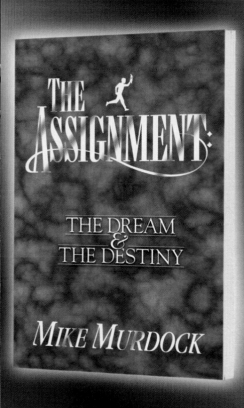

▶ 9 Keys In Making Your
Time Count...p.35-36

▶ 4 Rewards of Pain..p.39

▶ 14 Seasons In A
Minister's Life...p.49-50

▶ 15 Rewards For
Completing Your
Assignment...p.80-83

▶ The Benefits of
Crisis...p.91

▶ 12 Keys That
Unlock The Flow Of
Miracles...p.91-94

▶ 7 Important Keys In
Planning...p.121-122

▶ Importance Of
Anger...p.155-158

and much more!

• •

Everything that God created was created to solve a problem. The key to successful living is discovering the purpose for which you were created. This is your "Assignment." This Volume I on "The Dream & The Destiny" will unleash in you the discovery of our life calling. You will begin to know the joy of being in the center of God's will for your life!

Available also on six tapes for only $30!

Wisdom Is The Principal Thing

B-74

$10

6 Cassettes for $30

TS22

The Wisdom Center

PDB

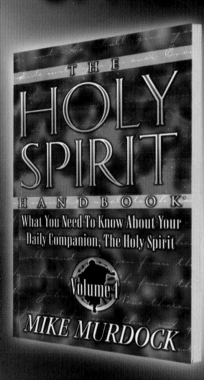

The 500 Billion Dollar Mar

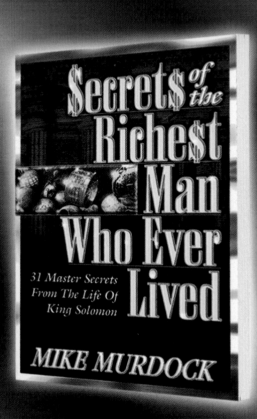

▶ **10 Important Facts You Should Recognize Abou Your Personal Limitations...p.25-30**

▶ **10 Qualities of Uncommon Achievers...p.37-41**

▶ **7 Keys To Help You Get Along With Others...p.50**

▶ **7 Immediate Steps You Take To Organize Your Dreams...p.62-63**

▶ **9 Negotiation Keys That Will Help Anyone Get W They Want...p.70-72**

▶ **7 Facts About Excellence That Could Change Your L Forever...p.84-86**

▶ **The Most Important Skill A Manager Can Possess...p.8**

...and muc more

Learning the secrets of great leaders should be a lifetime study. Dr. Murdock has invested hundreds of hours studying the life principles of the most successful individuals in the world from past to present. This teaching on the life of Solomon will bring you to a higher level of understanding in the secrets of uncommon wealth and success. God's best will soon be yours as you learn and put into practice these keys from the Richest Man Who Ever Lived!

Available also on six tapes for only $30!

Wisdom Is The Principal Thing

B-99
$10
6 Cassettes for $30
TS70

The Wisdom Center

PD

You Can Have It.

MIKE MURDOCK

▶ Why Sickness Is Not The Will of God…p.10

▶ How To Release The Powerful Forces That Guarantees Blessing…p.19

▶ The Incredible Role Of Your Memory & The Imagination…p.41

▶ The Hidden Power Of Imagination & How To Use It Properly…p.41

▶ The Difference Between The Love Of God And His Blessings…p.8

▶ 3 Steps In Increasing Your Faith…p.83

▶ 2 Rewards That come When You Use Your Faith In God…p.13

▶ 7 Powerful Keys Concerning Your Faith…p.78

…and much more!

Demands and desires as photographs within our hearts and minds - things that we want to happen in our future. God plants these pictures as invisible Seeds within us. God begins every miracle in your life with a Seed-picture…the invisible idea that gives birth to a visible blessing. In this teaching, you will discover your desires and how to concentrate on watering and nurturing the growth of your Dream-Seeds until you attain your God-given goals.

Available also on six tapes for only $30!

Wisdom Is The Principal Thing

B-11

$9

6 Cassettes for $30

TS2

The Wisdom Center

PDB

Something Incredible Is Very Close To You

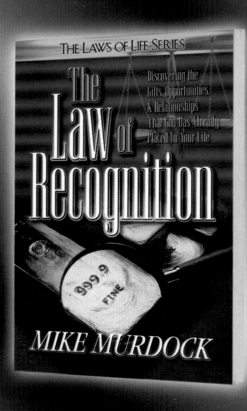

- ▶ 47 Keys In Recognizing The Mate God Has Approv For You…p.44-59

- ▶ 14 Facts You Should Know About Your Gifts and Talents…p.110-113

- ▶ 17 Important Facts You Should Remember About Your Weakness…p.166-168

- ▶ 10 Wisdom Keys That Changed My Life…p.118-12

- ▶ 24 Powerful Facts About The Uncommon Dream Within You…p.140-144

- ▶ 6 Facts You Should Know About Managing Your Time…p.210-211

- ▶ 46 Important Facts You Should Know About Problem-Solving…p.228-235

…and muc more

Anything Unrecognized Becomes Uncelebrated. Anything Uncelebrated Becomes Unrewarded. Anything Unrewarded Eventually Exits Your Life. The Law of Recognition can turn a lifetime of failure into instant success. God has provided storehouses of treasures around us and we need only to recognize it. In this teaching you'll learn to recognize the most important gifts in your life.

Wisdom Is The Principal Thing

B-114
$10

The Wisdom Center

PD

What Matters Most.

▶ 17 Facts You Should
   Know About The Holy
   Spirit…p.13-17

▶ The Greatest Weapon
   The Holy Spirit Has
   Given You…p.17

▶ 15 Facts About
   The Love Of The
   Holy Spirit…p.28-31

▶ 17 Facts Every Christian
   Should Know About
   Grieving The Holy
   Spirit…p.32-37

▶ 17 Facts You Should
   Know About The Anointing…p.60

▶ 3 Ways The Holy Spirit
   Will Talk To You…p.95-100

▶ 8 Important Facts
   About Your Assignment…p.83-84

…and much more!

•••••••••••••••••••••••••••••••••

The Holy Spirit, The Assignment, and The Seed. These three vital areas are the most important things in your life. Mike Murdock addresses each topic in a profound and dynamic way. In this volume he carefully lays out the Wisdom Secrets to Successful living. Your understanding will be energized as knowledge enters your heart and you begin to find your Assignment in the purpose of God. (232 pgs)

Wisdom Is The Principal Thing

B-101
$10

The Wisdom Center

PDB

Order Today!
The Wisdom Center • P.O. Box 99 • Denton, Texas • 76202
940 891 1400 • Fax: 940 891 4500 • www.mikemurdock.com

What Keeps Him Reaching

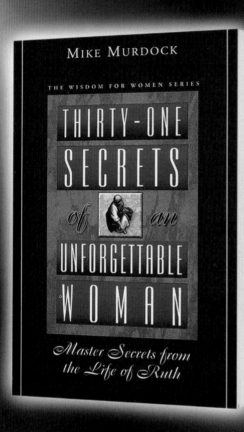

MIKE MURDOCK

THE WISDOM FOR WOMEN SERIES

THIRTY-ONE SECRETS of an UNFORGETTABLE WOMAN

Master Secrets from the Life of Ruth

▸ **How A Woman Can Predict The Success Of Her Man.**

▸ **What Every Uncommon Man Wishes Women Knew.**

▸ **The Most Magnetic Quality Men Look Fo In Women.**

▸ **The One Master Key To Understanding The Behavior Of A Man.**

▸ **What Attracts Wrong People In Your Life.**

▸ **The True Evidence That A Woman Possesses Integrity.**

▸ **Recognizing The Personality Flaw Guaranteed To Destroy Your Marriage.**

....*and muc mor*

Do you have big dreams? Are you willing to invest in those dreams? The story of Ruth in scripture is one example of a woman who was willing to invest in her present in order to have an extraordinary future.

Available also on six tapes for only $30!

Wisdom Is The Principal Thing

B-57
$10
6 Cassettes for $30
TS53

The Wisdom Center

PD

Order Today!
The Wisdom Center • P.O. Box 99 • Denton, Texas • 76202
940 891 1400 • Fax: 940 891 4500 • www.mikemurdock.com

W hen God wants to touch a nation, He raises up a preacher. It is Uncommon Men and Women of God who have driven back the darkness and shielded the unlearned and rebellious from devastation by satanic forces. They offer the breath of life to a dead world. They open Golden Doors to Change. They unleash The Forces of Truth in an age of deception.

Wisdom Is The Principal Thing

Code PAK UM1-7

$5ea

or All Seven for just

$25

The Wisdom Center

An Uncommon Minister is prepared through Seasons of Pain, Encounters with God, and Mentors. Having sat at the feet of Uncommon Mentors his entire life, Dr. Mike Murdock shares practical but personal keys to increase the excellence and productivity of your ministry. Each volume of "The Uncommon Minister" is handy, convenient and easy to read. Your load will be lighter, your journey happier, and your effectiveness increased in "doing the will of the Father."

PDB

Order Today!
The Wisdom Center • P.O. Box 99 • Denton, Texas • 76202
940 891 1400 • Fax: 940 891 4500 • www.mikemurdock.com

THE SECRET PLACE PAK

VOLUME 13

Wisdom Is The Principal Thing

Cassettes & Book for only

$30

A $35 Value

The Wisdom Center

Songs from the Secret Place	40 great songs on 6 Tapes Includes "Everything I Need I Get In Your Prsence", "Fill This Place With Your Presence".
Seeds of Wisdom on The Secret Place	10 Facts Every Believer Should Know About the Secret Place (PAK-001)

PD

Order Today!
The Wisdom Center • P.O. Box 99 • Denton, Texas • 76202
940.891.1400 • Fax: 940.891.4500 • www.mikemurdock.com

WISDOM COLLECTION

1

The Greatest Secret of the Universe

Collection Includes:
1. The Greatest Secret of the Universe (Six Cassettes)
2. The Holy Spirit Handbook (Six Cassettes)
3. Songs From the Secret Place (Six Music Cassettes)
4. The Holy Spirit—The Greatest Secret of the Universe (Video)
5. The Jesus Book (173 Page Book)
6. The Holy Spirit Handbook (166 Page Book)
7. 12 Seeds of Wisdom Books On 12 Topics
8. The Gift of Wisdom for Champions Desk Calendar
9. In Honor of the Holy Spirit (Music Cassette)
10. The Mentor's Manna—The Secret Place (Audio Cassette)

Wisdom Is The Principal Thing
Code WC101
Gift of Appreciation
For Any Seed of
$200
Or More To Our Ministry
The Wisdom Center

PDB

Order Today!
The Wisdom Center • P.O. Box 99 • Denton, Texas • 76202
940 891 1400 • Fax: 940 891 4500 • www.mikemurdock.com

WISDOM COLLECTION

8

SECRETS OF THE UNCOMMON MILLIONAIRE

1. The Uncommon Millionaire Conference Vol. 1 (Six Cassettes)
2. The Uncommon Millionaire Conference Vol. 2 (Six Cassettes)
3. The Uncommon Millionaire Conference Vol. 3 (Six Cassettes)
4. The Uncommon Millionaire Conference Vol. 4 (Six Cassettes)
5. 31 Reasons People Do Not Receive Their
   Financial Harvest (256 Page Book)
6. Secrets of the Richest Man Who Ever Lived
   (178 Page Book)
7. 12 Seeds of Wisdom Books On 12 Topics
8. The Gift of Wisdom for Leaders Desk Calendar
9. Songs From The Secret Place (Music Cassette)
10. In Honor of the Holy Spirit (Music Cassette)
11. 365 Memorization Scriptures On The Word Of God (Audio Cassette)

PD

Wisdom Is The Principal Thing

Code WC108
Gift of Appreciation
For Any Seed of

$200

Or More To Our Ministry

The Wisdom Center

YOU WILL NEVER BE THE SAME

The School Of Wisdom Collection

Wisdom Is The Principal Thing

Each Volume contains 6 Cassettes for $30 All 4 for only $99

The Wisdom Center

Thousands are being mentored through these life-changing Conference tapes. Dr. Mike Murdock deals with many topics including the Holy Spirit, Financial Breakthrough, Time Management Techniques, Goal Setting, Negotiation, People Pressure, Focus, The Law of Order, Unleashing Favor and many more.

• The Uncommon Life (TS 85)
• 101 Wisdom Keys That Have Changed My Life (TS 90)
• What I'd Do Differently If I Could Begin My Life Over Again (TS 83)
• Unleashing Uncommon Favor (TS 89)
• School Of Wisdom - All 4 Only $99 (TS PAK001)

PDB

Order Today!
The Wisdom Center • P.O. Box 99 • Denton, Texas • 76202
940 891 1400 • Fax: 940-891-4500 • www.mikemurdock.com

Desktop Mentors.

- A 31 Days Mentorship Program
- A great gift for any occasion
- Use it as your Daily Mentor
- Success Keys for each subject
- A Scripture for each day of the Mont

THE 31 DAY MENTORSHIP PROGRAM

The Gift Of Wisdom for Leaders

31 Wisdom Keys For Each Day Of The Month

MIKE MURDOCK

Day-15

The Uncommon Leader Refuses To Give Up His Dream.

Failures happen. Mistakes are common. But God is the God of the second chance. He will always outlast your storms. *Always.* The Uncommon Leader knows this. So, he encourages others to stop looking at where they have been and start looking at where they are going. He knows the incredible power of dreaming again.

"The glory of this latter house shall be greater than of the former; saith the Lord of hosts: and in this place will I give peace, saith the Lord of hosts" (Haggai 2:9).

The Gift Of Wisdom for Champions — MIKE MURDOCK

The Gift Of Wisdom for Ministers — MIKE MURDOCK

The Gift Of Wisdom for Brides — MIKE MURDOCK

The Gift Of Wisdom for Grooms — MIKE MURDOCK

The Gift Of Wisdom for Fathers — MIKE MURDOCK

The Gift Of Wisdom for Teenagers — MIKE MURDOCK

The Gift Of Wisdom for Graduates — MIKE MURDOCK

The Gift Of Wisdom for Mothers — MIKE MURDOCK

Wisdom Is The Principal Thing
ONLY $8 EACH
The Wisdom Center

- ACHIEVERS • BRIDES • CHAMPIONS • FATHERS • GRADUATES • GROOMS
- HUSBANDS • LEADERS • MINISTERS • MOTHERS • TEENAGERS • WIVES

This 31 Day Desktop Mentor can be placed anywhere that you work, play or study. It is designed to help you focus your attention on the Wisdom of God. Use it as your daily Mentor and watch these Seeds of Wisdom bring you a harvest of success. You can order other titles for your family and friends.

PD